P9-BZC-820

DATE DUE

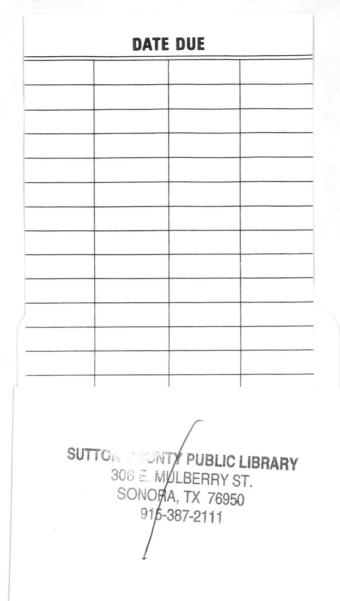

5

Great
Hispanics
of Our Time

Joan Baez:
Folksinger for Peace

Maritza Romero

The Rosen Publishing Group's
PowerKids Press™
New York

Published in 1997 by The Rosen Publishing Group, Inc.
29 East 21st Street, New York, NY 10010

First Edition

Book Design: Danielle Primiceri

Photo Credits: Cover © Patrick Balloul/Archive Photos; pp. 4, 7, 8 (left inset), 11, 12, 19 © AP/Wide World Photos; p. 8 (background and right inset) © J. Baptiste/Viesti Associates; pp. 15, 16 (all insets), 20 (background and inset) © Archive Photos; p. 16 (background) © Ed Hoy/FPG International; p. 19 (inset) © Bettmann.

Romero, Maritza.
    Joan Baez : folksinger / Maritza Romero.
        p.   cm. — (Great Hispanics of our time)
    Summary: A biography of the Mexican American folksinger who became a political activist and who wrote and sang songs that inspired people to make the world better.
    ISBN 0-8239-5084-0
    1. Baez, Joan—Juvenile literature. 2. Singers—United States—Biography—Juvenile literature. [1. Baez, Joan.   2. Mexican Americans—Biography. 3. Singers. 4. Political activists. 5. Women—Biography.] I. Title. II. Series.
ML3930.B205R66 1997
782.42162'0092
[B]—DC21
                                                  97-7432
                                                  CIP
                                                  AC

Manufactured in the United States of America

Contents

Filled with Music

Joan Chandos Baez was born on January 9, 1941, on Staten Island, New York. Her mother was Scottish and her father was Mexican. Her father worked as a **physicist** (FIZ-ih-sist). He changed jobs often, so the family moved around a lot. But Joan spent most of her childhood in California.

The Baez home was always filled with music. The family listened to **classical** (CLASS-ih-kul) music while they ate dinner, and they listened to the radio during the rest of the day.

◀ Joan Baez had no idea that she would become a world-famous singer when she grew up.

Something to Believe In

As a child, Joan learned that if you believe strongly in something, you should do something about it. Joan's parents became **Quakers** (KWAY-kerz) when Joan and her two sisters were young. Quakers believe that people should not use **violence** (VY-uh-lents) against each other, especially in war.

When Joan's father was asked to help make military airplanes, he said no. He could have been rich, but he decided not to work on something he believed was wrong. Instead, he became a college professor.

The Baez family believed strongly that people should not fight in wars. ▶

Joan Learns a Lesson

When Joan was nine, her father took a job at the University of Baghdad in Iraq. The whole family moved to Iraq for a year. In Baghdad, Joan saw many people suffering. She saw people searching through garbage for food. She saw children her own age who were very sick and living on the streets. It was something she would never forget. Joan knew that she wanted to help make the world a better place for people.

◀ While she was in Baghdad, Joan saw the beautiful sights as well as the suffering of many of the people.

Having a Hard Time

When the Baez family returned to California in 1951, Joan had trouble in school. Because her name, skin color, and hair color showed that she was Hispanic, the white kids didn't accept her. But because she didn't speak Spanish, the Mexican kids didn't accept her either. So Joan had few friends.

Joan had another problem. She always said what was on her mind. Not everyone liked that. Like her parents, she did not think that war was a good thing, and she said so. Other students and their parents called Joan a troublemaker.

Joan was never afraid to say what she thought. Many people liked this about her. Others did not. ▶

Joan Learns to Sing

Joan was very lonely. She thought that people might like her better if she could sing. So she tried out for the school glee club, which is a club just for singing songs. Joan was told that she didn't sing very well. But she didn't give up. She taught herself to sing better and to play the guitar. Soon Joan was singing beautifully for her school and her new friends. Each time her father changed jobs, Joan used her singing as a way to make new friends.

◀ Joan didn't let other people stop her from reaching her goal of learning how to sing.

Becoming a Folksinger

When Joan finished high school in 1958, the Baez family moved to Cambridge, Massachusetts. One night, Joan's father took the family to a coffeehouse where **folksingers** (FOHK-sing-erz) sang.

Soon Joan was singing and playing her guitar there too. She sang songs from all over the world. At first, she only sang sad songs. But soon she learned to sing funny songs, and to joke and laugh with her **audience** (AW-dee-ents). People loved listening to Joan.

Joan enjoyed performing for other people. ▶

A Star Is Born

Joan was invited to sing at the Newport Folk Festival in Rhode Island in 1959. The audience cheered for her music. The next year, she recorded an album with a record company. The album was called *Joan Baez*. It became the third most popular album in the country. At the time, it was the best-selling record for a woman folksinger and for a Hispanic person.

Joan was a star. Everyone wanted her to perform at concerts and make more records.

◀ Joan recorded several albums and gave many concerts. Sometimes she performed with other famous singers, such as Bob Dylan.

Teaching Through Music

Joan began to use her music to teach others about things that she thought were wrong. She sang many **protest** (PRO-test) songs about the Vietnam War, in which the United States was fighting. She also sang out against **racism** (RAY-sizm). She joined **civil rights** (SIH-vul RYTS) leader Dr. Martin Luther King, Jr., in many marches. She sang her songs to the crowds that gathered to hear Dr. King speak. In 1965, Joan and some friends opened a school in California called the Institute for the Study of Nonviolence. They taught people how to protest without using violence.

Like Dr. Martin Luther King, Jr., Joan believed in equal rights and nonviolence. ▶

Singing for Peace

Many people protested the Vietnam War. In 1968, Joan, with other protestors, was put in jail for two weeks. In 1969, Joan and other musicians played at a music festival in Woodstock, New York. It was about peace, love, and ending the war. In 1972, Joan was invited by the North Vietnamese to see what was happening in North Vietnam. Joan recorded an album about the suffering that she saw there. She wanted to tell others about the pain and sadness the Vietnamese people faced during the war. The war didn't end until 1975.

◀ Many people agreed with Joan's songs about having peace and ending the Vietnam War.

Music to Believe In

Joan Baez still has fans all over the world. She writes and sings songs that **inspire** (in-SPYR) people to make the world a better place to live in. Joan's songs give hope during bad times.

Joan has recorded 32 albums, and is still singing today. People **admire** (ad-MYR) Joan's music, and her example of always doing what you believe in.

Glossary

admire (ad-MYR) To like someone very much.

audience (AW-dee-ents) A group of people gathered to watch or listen to someone or something.

civil rights (SIH-vul RYTS) The rights of every person in the United States.

classical (CLASS-ih-kul) A style of music that is mostly instrumental.

folksinger (FOHK-sing-er) A person who sings music about people and events.

inspire (in-SPYR) To fill with a wish to do or say something.

physicist (FIZ-ih-sist) A person who studies the way things work.

protest (PRO-test) To speak out about something you think is wrong.

Quaker (KWAY-ker) A member of a Christian group that takes part in simple religious services and does not believe in war or the use of violence.

racism (RAY-sizm) The mistaken belief that one race or group of people is better than another.

violence (VY-uh-lents) Strong, harmful force.

Index